PEACE THAT EXCEEDS

Dear Reader,

I designed this prayer tool out of necessity for myself. After becoming a mom in 2011, my blank prayer journals began collecting dust because of exhaustion. Writing out long prayers and having any blocks of time alone became a thing of the past. In 2015, we moved to Papua New Guinea as a family to become church planters and began an even busier season of learning a trade language and eventually a tribal language.

I knew I needed a change to stay focused in prayer!

I needed help in remembering what needs I wanted to pray for my family, friends, church members, and all the heaviness in this world. How many times have you told someone you'd pray for them and forgot what that was?

This journal was born of that busy season. It's for those in their own busy season, the grieving or distracted, those living in fear and crippled by worry, and anyone wanting to have more focused prayer time.

I pray that it will focus your prayers too! May He give you the peace that comes with turning everything over to Him in prayer.

With love,
Jinny Richards

USING THIS PRAYER JOURNAL

Take some time at the beginning of each month to think about each prompt and write down what you need to pray about in that category. Then, when you take time for prayer, pray through at least one prompt or more. This journal is designed to help you focus so that you're not left forgetting what to pray for when you do have the time for it. It is small enough to keep in a bag and will be available when that friend asks you to pray for something and you don't want to forget about it!

At the end of the month, take some time to thank God and write your answered prayers, and the Scripture He's used to impact you. Be encouraged as you go back to months past to remember His faithfulness!

MONTH, YEAR

PERSONAL GROWTH
Areas in which I need to grow.

GRATITUDE
Things for which I am grateful.

MY FAMILY & FRIENDS
Prayers for my spouse, kids, parents, friends, etc.

BODY OF CHRIST

Prayers for my church leaders, small group or Bible study members, local ministries, etc.

WORRIES, ANXIETIES & BURDENS
"Do not worry about anything. Instead, pray!"

_____

_____
_____
_____
_____

SALVATION
Prayers for unbelievers in my life.

_____

_____
_____
_____
_____

MISSIONARIES
Ask God to send more laborers into the field. Pray for missionaries that I know or support, and for unreached people groups.

_____

_____
_____
_____
_____

DECISIONS

_____

_____
_____
_____
_____

SCRIPTURES
Verses that impacted me this month.

_____

_____
_____
_____
_____

PERSONALIZED CATEGORIES
Suggestions: marriage, school, job or finances.

_____

_____
_____
_____
_____

PERSONALIZED CATEGORIES
Suggestions: marriage, school, job or finances.

PERSONALIZED CATEGORIES
Suggestions: marriage, school, job or finances.

ANSWERED PRAYERS

MONTH, YEAR

PERSONAL GROWTH
Areas in which I need to grow.

GRATITUDE
Things for which I am grateful.

MY FAMILY & FRIENDS
Prayers for my spouse, kids, parents, friends, etc.

BODY OF CHRIST

Prayers for my church leaders, small group or Bible study members, local ministries, etc.

WORRIES, ANXIETIES & BURDENS
"Do not worry about anything. Instead, pray!"

_____

_____

_____

_____

_____

SALVATION
Prayers for unbelievers in my life.

_____

_____

_____

_____

_____

MISSIONARIES
Ask God to send more laborers into the field. Pray for missionaries that I know or support, and for unreached people groups.

_____

_____

_____

_____

_____

DECISIONS

SCRIPTURES
Verses that impacted me this month.

PERSONALIZED CATEGORIES
Suggestions: marriage, school, job or finances.

PERSONALIZED CATEGORIES
Suggestions: marriage, school, job or finances.

PERSONALIZED CATEGORIES
Suggestions: marriage, school, job or finances.

ANSWERED PRAYERS

MONTH, YEAR

PERSONAL GROWTH
Areas in which I need to grow.

GRATITUDE
Things for which I am grateful.

MY FAMILY & FRIENDS
Prayers for my spouse, kids, parents, friends, etc.

BODY OF CHRIST

Prayers for my church leaders, small group or Bible study members, local ministries, etc.

WORRIES, ANXIETIES & BURDENS
"Do not worry about anything. Instead, pray!"

SALVATION
Prayers for unbelievers in my life.

MISSIONARIES
Ask God to send more laborers into the field. Pray for missionaries that I know or support, and for unreached people groups.

DECISIONS

SCRIPTURES
Verses that impacted me this month.

PERSONALIZED CATEGORIES
Suggestions: marriage, school, job or finances.

PERSONALIZED CATEGORIES
Suggestions: marriage, school, job or finances.

PERSONALIZED CATEGORIES
Suggestions: marriage, school, job or finances.

ANSWERED PRAYERS

MONTH, YEAR

PERSONAL GROWTH
Areas in which I need to grow.

GRATITUDE
Things for which I am grateful.

MY FAMILY & FRIENDS
Prayers for my spouse, kids, parents, friends, etc.

BODY OF CHRIST

Prayers for my church leaders, small group or Bible study members, local ministries, etc.

WORRIES, ANXIETIES & BURDENS
"Do not worry about anything. Instead, pray!"

_____

_____
_____
_____
_____

SALVATION
Prayers for unbelievers in my life.

_____

_____
_____
_____
_____

MISSIONARIES
Ask God to send more laborers into the field. Pray for missionaries that I know or support, and for unreached people groups.

_____

_____
_____
_____
_____

DECISIONS

SCRIPTURES
Verses that impacted me this month.

PERSONALIZED CATEGORIES
Suggestions: marriage, school, job or finances.

PERSONALIZED CATEGORIES
Suggestions: marriage, school, job or finances.

PERSONALIZED CATEGORIES
Suggestions: marriage, school, job or finances.

ANSWERED PRAYERS

MONTH, YEAR

PERSONAL GROWTH
Areas in which I need to grow.

GRATITUDE
Things for which I am grateful.

MY FAMILY & FRIENDS
Prayers for my spouse, kids, parents, friends, etc.

BODY OF CHRIST

Prayers for my church leaders, small group or Bible study members, local ministries, etc.

WORRIES, ANXIETIES & BURDENS
"Do not worry about anything. Instead, pray!"

_____

_____

_____

_____

_____

SALVATION
Prayers for unbelievers in my life.

_____

_____

_____

_____

_____

MISSIONARIES
Ask God to send more laborers into the field. Pray for missionaries that I know or support, and for unreached people groups.

_____

_____

_____

_____

_____

DECISIONS

SCRIPTURES
Verses that impacted me this month.

PERSONALIZED CATEGORIES
Suggestions: marriage, school, job or finances.

PERSONALIZED CATEGORIES
Suggestions: marriage, school, job or finances.

PERSONALIZED CATEGORIES
Suggestions: marriage, school, job or finances.

ANSWERED PRAYERS

MONTH, YEAR

PERSONAL GROWTH
Areas in which I need to grow.

GRATITUDE
Things for which I am grateful.

MY FAMILY & FRIENDS
Prayers for my spouse, kids, parents, friends, etc.

BODY OF CHRIST

Prayers for my church leaders, small group or Bible study members, local ministries, etc.

WORRIES, ANXIETIES & BURDENS
"Do not worry about anything. Instead, pray!"

_____

_____

_____

_____

_____

SALVATION
Prayers for unbelievers in my life.

_____

_____

_____

_____

_____

MISSIONARIES
Ask God to send more laborers into the field. Pray for missionaries that I know or support, and for unreached people groups.

_____

_____

_____

_____

_____

DECISIONS

SCRIPTURES
Verses that impacted me this month.

PERSONALIZED CATEGORIES
Suggestions: marriage, school, job or finances.

PERSONALIZED CATEGORIES
Suggestions: marriage, school, job or finances.

PERSONALIZED CATEGORIES
Suggestions: marriage, school, job or finances.

ANSWERED PRAYERS

ANSWERED PRAYERS

ANSWERED PRAYERS

ANSWERED PRAYERS

THIS JOURNAL BELONGS TO

_____

DATES

_____

TO

CLICK QR TO ORDER REPLACEMENT JOURNALS

©2022 Tapestry Books
ISBN: 9781629442020

www.ingramcontent.com/pod-product-compliance
Lightning Source LLC
Chambersburg PA
CBHW020443090526
44586CB00045B/829